THE THREE Rs

REDUCE, REUSE, AND RECYCLE

PAPER

Jared Siemens

Lightbox is an all-inclusive digital solution for the teaching and learning of curriculum topics in an original, groundbreaking way. Lightbox is based on National Curriculum Standards.

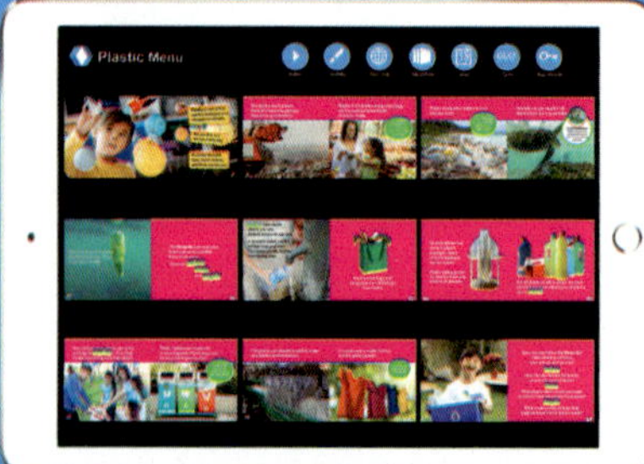

OPTIMIZED FOR

- ✓ TABLETS
- ✓ WHITEBOARDS
- ✓ COMPUTERS
- ✓ AND MUCH MORE!

STANDARD FEATURES OF LIGHTBOX

 **AUDIO** High-quality narration using text-to-speech system

 **VIDEOS** Embedded high-definition video clips

 **ACTIVITIES** Printable PDFs that can be emailed and graded

 **WEBLINKS** Curated links to external, child-safe resources

 **SLIDESHOWS** Pictorial overviews of key concepts

 **INTERACTIVE MAPS** Interactive maps and aerial satellite imagery

 **QUIZZES** Ten multiple choice questions that are automatically graded and emailed for teacher assessment

 **KEY WORDS** Matching key concepts to their definitions

VIDEOS

WEBLINKS

SLIDESHOWS

QUIZZES

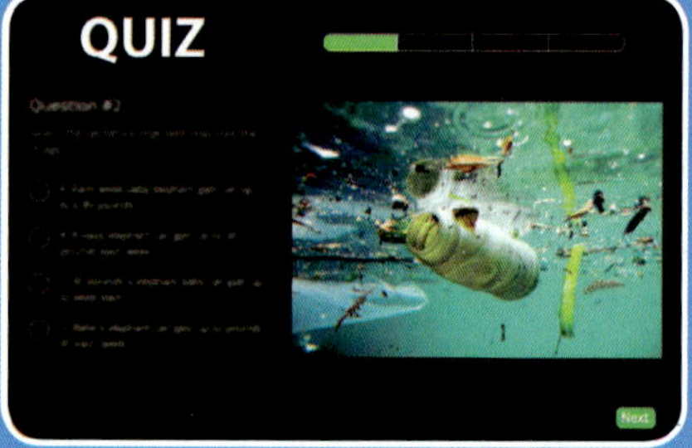

In this book, you will learn

what paper is,

how it affects Earth,

how it is wasted,

how you can help,

and much more!

Paper is a natural material. It is a very important part of daily life.

We use paper when we read a book, write a note, and draw a picture.

It can be found in textbooks, tissues, and cereal boxes.

People use enormous amounts of paper. From newspapers to lunch bags, paper is everywhere.

We throw out too much paper. We send more paper to the landfill each year than any other kind of waste.

People **throw away** enough **toilet paper** tubes **each year** to fill **two Empire State Buildings**.

Paper is made from trees. Trees have to be cut down and ground up to make paper.

Each American uses about **seven trees** of paper **each year**.

Cutting down too many trees can hurt Earth. Trees clean our air and help keep Earth cool.

Georgia makes **more paper** than any other state. Its **forests** could cover **New York City** more than **100 times**.

We need to work together to save trees and make paper last.

The **Three Rs** is an easy plan that helps us do just that. It has three steps.

These are reduce, reuse, and recycle.

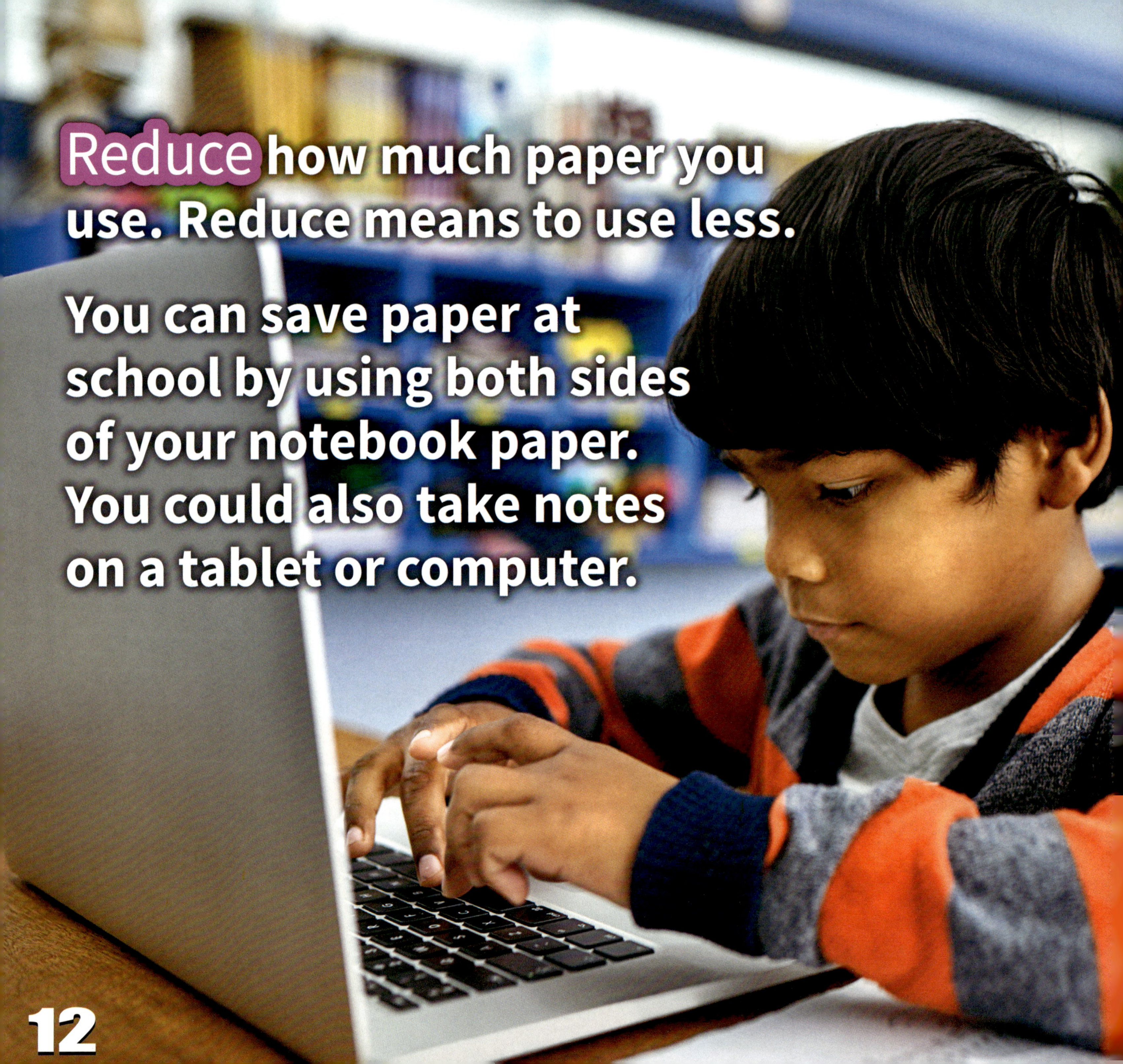

Reduce how much paper you use. Reduce means to use less.

You can save paper at school by using both sides of your notebook paper. You could also take notes on a tablet or computer.

At home, you can use a cloth to wipe up spills instead of paper towel.

You can reduce paper use in all kinds of ways.

A used newspaper can be put into wet sneakers to help them dry.

You can reuse old note paper to make your own recycled paper. Ask a parent or teacher for help.

You can keep paper out of the garbage by **recycling** it. More than 260 million Americans have paper recycling bins.

Computer paper you recycle today may become tomorrow's paper towel.

Enough paper is recycled in the **United States each day** to fill a **15-mile** (24-kilometer) **long train** of boxcars.

Today, people want to replace plastic with paper. Plastic straws hurt ocean animals when they are thrown away.

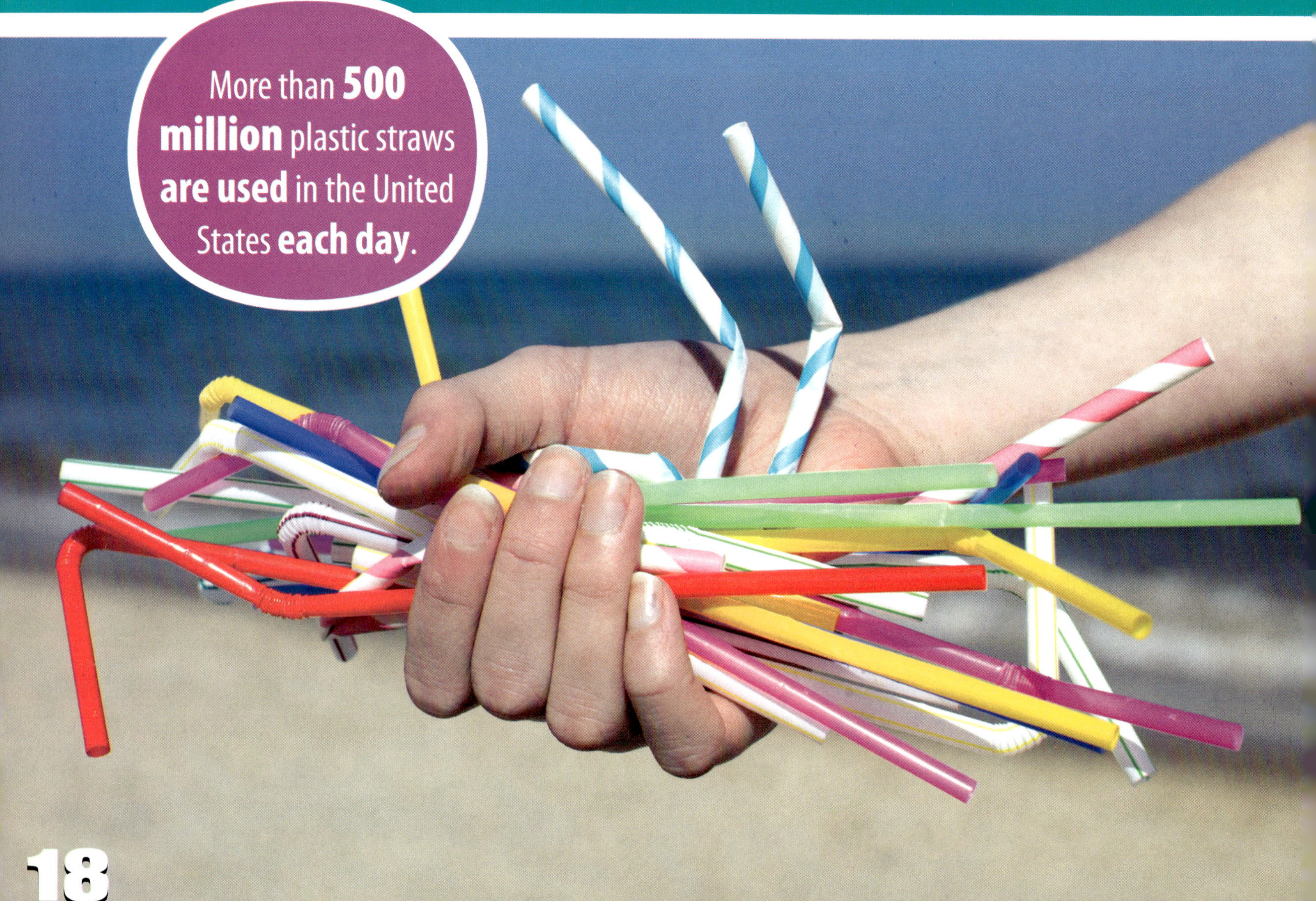

More than **500 million** plastic straws **are used** in the United States **each day**.

Paper straws are much better. They break down when they are thrown away.

How can you follow the **Three Rs**? Think about your home, your school, and your neighborhood.

Reduce

What ways do you use paper each day? How might you use less paper?

Reuse

What kinds of paper could you reuse at school? How would you reuse it?

Recycle

What kinds of paper do you throw out? How could you recycle more paper at home?

PAPER FACTS

These pages provide detailed information that expands on the interesting facts found in the book. They are intended to be used by adults as a learning support to help young readers round out their knowledge of reducing, reusing, or recycling each kind of object or material featured in *The Three Rs* series.

Pages 4–5

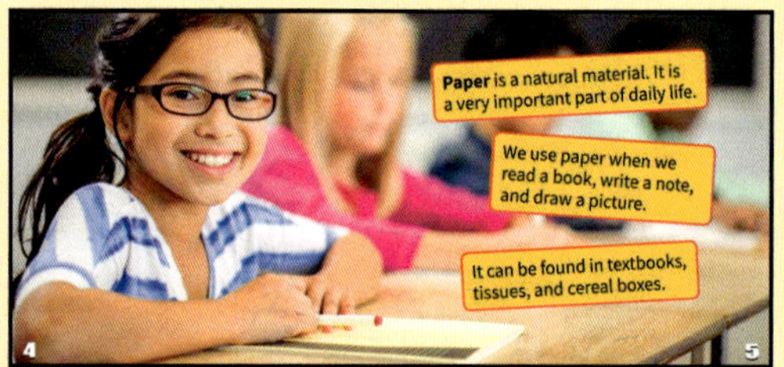

Paper was invented by Cai Lun in China nearly 2,000 years ago. From the early days of the printing press in the 15th century to now, paper has transformed people's ability to share and record thoughts, feelings, and ideas. Even with the push to go paperless, paper is still important to people and businesses alike. Contracts, university degrees, certificates, and other official documents are still printed on paper.

Pages 6–7

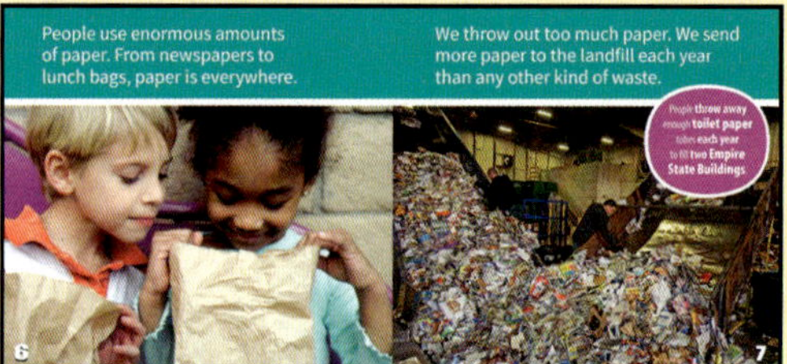

In the United States, people use about 85 million tons (77 million metric tons) of paper and paper products each year. That is about 680 pounds (310 kilograms) per person, or just a little more than the weight of a grand piano. Americans throw away about 1 billion trees' worth of paper each year. Paper and paper items account for the largest percentage of municipal waste sent to the landfill. What might happen to trees in the United States if people keep using paper this way?

Pages 8–9

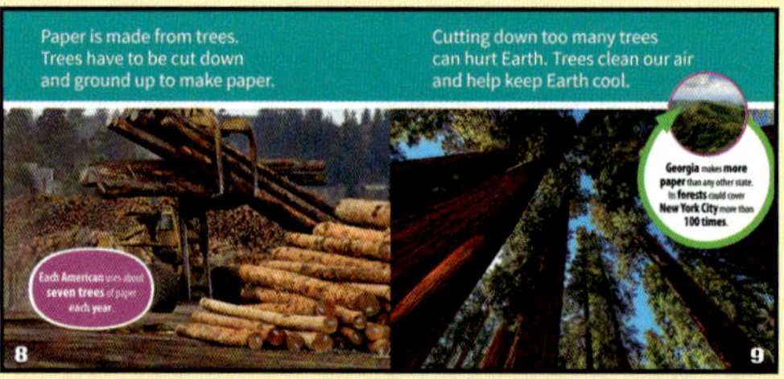

Paper is made by mixing ground wood fibers with water. Then, these fibers are pressed against a screen to filter out the water. As the fibers dry together, a sheet of paper is formed. Around the world, nearly 11 million trees are cut down every single day to make paper. Trees do the important job of producing oxygen and absorbing carbon dioxide. Carbon dioxide makes Earth's air heat up. Without trees to absorb carbon dioxide, what could happen to the temperatures on Earth?

Pages 10–11

The United States uses about 26 percent of the world's overall paper pulp. This means reducing, reusing, and recycling paper is very important in the United States. When you buy paper, toilet paper, or tissues, look for the Forest Stewardship Council logo. This symbol means the FSC ensures the paper product came from a well-managed forest. It may also mean the product came from recycled materials.

Pages 12–13

Reducing paper use can be done in a variety of ways. When you get food from a restaurant with your family, eat at the restaurant instead of taking it out. This saves you from using a paper bag, napkins, and take-out containers that the food would have come in. When you are shopping, you can ask for your receipt to be sent by email. Your parents can also request that their monthly bills be sent electronically instead of by mail to save paper.

Pages 14–15

Newspaper is designed to absorb moisture. This helps ink stick to it. It also enables newspaper to absorb smells and moisture from wet shoes and reusable food containers. You can also use scrap paper and junk mail to make your own paper. First, tear the paper into small pieces and soak it in water. Then, have a parent or teacher blend it to pulp in a blender. Flatten the pulp on a screen and allow it to dry completely. Then, carefully peel away your sheet of paper from the screen.

Pages 16–17

Recycled paper is pulped in a mix of chemicals at a paper mill. Chemicals help separate the paper fibers. Then, other contaminants, such as glues and staples, are filtered out. The pulp is then sent to another tank, where more chemicals clean the paper to remove ink. One piece of paper can be recycled as many as seven times. Making paper from recycled paper uses far less energy and water than making paper from raw materials. More than 87 percent of Americans have access to paper recycling.

Pages 18–19

More than 8 million tons (7.26 metric tons) of plastic goes into the ocean each year. This amount of plastic could make 3.4 quadrillion 2x4 LEGO bricks. This is enough LEGO bricks to build 19 life-size Empire State Buildings. In 2018, the European Union proposed a bill to forbid disposable plastic items, including straws, in all the 28 member countries. Like paper towels, most paper straws can be composted following use.

Pages 20–21

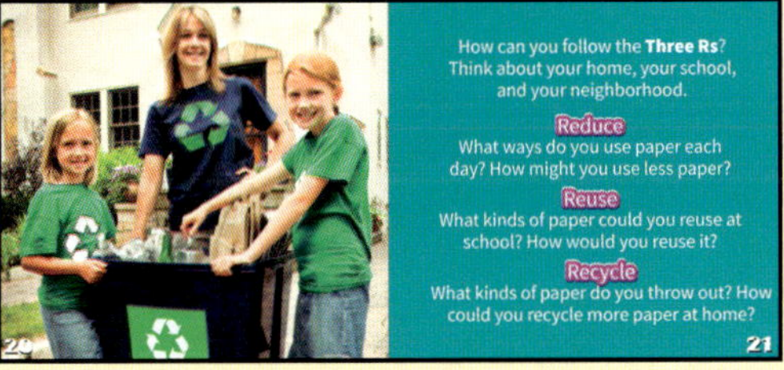

In 2016, the United States recycled a record-breaking 67.2 percent of its paper. Thanks to paper recycling and sustainable forestry initiatives, the United States has 20 percent more trees today than it did on the first Earth Day in 1970. While recycling paper is good for trees, it is not always good for people. Studies show paper recycling mills use starches that can make a bacterial slime. This bacteria, which is similar to the kind that causes food poisoning, can end up in recycled paper products and make people sick.

KEY WORDS

Research has shown that as much as 65 percent of all written material published in English is made up of 300 words. These 300 words cannot be taught using pictures or learned by sounding them out. They must be recognized by sight. This book contains 105 common sight words to help young readers improve their reading fluency and comprehension. This book also teaches young readers several important content words, such as proper nouns. These words are paired with pictures to aid in learning and improve understanding.

Page	Sight Words First Appearance
5	a, and, be, book, can, found, important, in, is, it, life, of, paper, part, picture, read, use, very, we, when, write
6	from, people, to
7	any, away, each, enough, kind, more, much, other, out, than, the, too, two, year
8	about, American, cut, down, have, made, trees, up
9	air, could, Earth, help, its, keep, makes, many, new, our, state, times
10	last, need, together, work
11	an, are, do, has, just, that, these, three, us
12	also, at, both, by, how, means, on, or, school, sides, take, you, your
13	home
14	all, into, put, them, ways
15	ask, for, old, own
17	day, long, may, mile
18	they, want, with
21	might, think, what, would

Page	Content Words First Appearance
5	cereal boxes, material, note, textbook,tissues
6	lunch bags, newspapers
7	Empire State Building, landfill, toilet paper tubes, waste
9	forests, Georgia, New York City
11	plant, recycle, reduce, reuse, steps, Three Rs
12	computer, notebook paper, tablet
13	cloth, paper towel, spills
14	sneakers
15	parent, recycled paper, teacher
16	garbage, recycling bins
17	boxcars, today, tomorrow, train, United States
18	plastic straws
21	neighborhood

Published by Smartbook Media Inc.
350 5th Avenue, 59th Floor New York, NY 10118
Website: www.openlightbox.com

Library of Congress Control Number: 2018941512

ISBN 978-1-5105-3805-4 (hardcover)
ISBN 978-1-5105-3806-1 (multi-user eBook)

062018
120117

Printed in Brainerd, Minnesota, United States
1 2 3 4 5 6 7 8 9 0 22 21 20 19 18

Project Coordinator: Jared Siemens
Designer: Terry Paulhus

Every reasonable effort has been made to trace ownership and to obtain permission to reprint copyright material. The publisher would be pleased to have any errors or omissions brought to its attention so that they may be corrected in subsequent printings.

The publisher acknowledges Alamy, Getty Images, iStock, Shutterstock, and Dreamstime as its primary image suppliers for this title.